When the Sun Was a Poet

A Lyrical Almanac of Life's
Seasons and Seasonings

When the Sun Was a Poet

A Lyrical Almanac of Life's Seasons and Seasonings

Poetry by

Jill Y. Crainshaw

© 2025 Jill Y. Crainshaw. All rights reserved.
This material may not be reproduced in any form, published,
reprinted, recorded, performed, broadcast,
rewritten, or redistributed without
the explicit permission of Jill Y. Crainshaw.
All such actions are strictly prohibited by law.

Cover design by Shay Culligan
Cover image by Sheila G. Hunter
Author photo by Roger Epps

ISBN: 978-1-63980-694-2
Library of Congress Control Number: 2025930530

Kelsay Books
502 South 1040 East, A-119
American Fork, Utah 84003
Kelsaybooks.com

Acknowledgments

The author wishes to acknowledge the editors of the following publications in which some of the poems in this collection first appeared:

The Graveyard Literary Zine: "Sacramental Seasons"
North Carolina Bards Anthology: "a murder of winter stillness"
Patheos: "Cedars in Snowy Places"
The Poet's Billow: "vital signs"
Poets Reading the News: "The Other Half of the Sky"
Rockvale Review: "Colors Against the Night"
Synkdroniciti: "Tombstone Tales"
What Rough Beast: "Dear Midnight"
Within and Without Magazine: "life as we know it"

Contents

Prologue

When the Sun Was a Poet   15

I. Spring's Dawning Cry

Sowing Kisses into the Wind   19
Snow Peas   20
caterpillar stitches   21
Mockingbird Remix   22
in the eye of the beholder   24
with our eyes on the sparrows   25
Letter to Last Spring's Robin   26
rocking chair   27
Tombstone Tales   29

II. Summer's Sun-Soaked Rhapsody

sacramental season   33
Red Deck Chairs on an Old Back Deck   35
dark roast on a summer sabbath   37
Colors Against the Night   38
Summer Dance   39
a storied plot in a summertime backyard   40
the white and silver hearse   41
Hummingbird Blessing   43

III. Autumn's Luminescent Lyric

First Day of Autumn   47
A Ginkgo at Thanksgiving   48
Harvest Gifts   49

October Offering	51
ode to a sycamore	52
Ashes to Ashes	53
Winter Prelude	55

IV. Winter's Silver-Sheened Silences

Cedars in Snowy Places	59
Upon a Midnight	60
i want my feet to tell me	62
a murder of stillness	63
silenced snow globe	64
winter pilgrimage	65
January Epiphanies	66

V. Celestial Dances

Daffodil Prayers	71
On Not Chasing Time	73
to "watch again another night"	74
Newborn Lullabies	75
vital signs	77
Beneath Our Feet, In Our Hands	79
harvesting ancient sunrises	80
Dear Midnight,	81
Saving a Dance for Me	83
The Other Half of the Sky	84

Epilogue: the sun is a poet

Prologue

The Sun warms the earth and our bodies. She boosts our energy and lifts our spirits. Trees and plants feast on the Sun's rays to live and grow. With every bite and breath, we synthesize sunlight into the bones and sinews and marrow of our lives. The Sun infuses the dust of the earth with light and illumines human spirits.

The Sun celebrates seasons too. As she and the earth choreograph their celestial dance, she comes to us robed in autumn's burnt sienna, winter's silver-blue sheen, spring's dazzling cadmium yellow, and summer's bold and juicy gold. Sometimes we cannot miss her radiant presence. At other times, she settles into our lives as a circumspect sage.

When the Sun Was a Poet leans in to look and listen for the Sun's lyrical and life-giving gifts and to reveal unexpected places where the Sun's poetry enlivens and enlightens our life seasons. The collection traces the Sun's sometimes dazzling, sometimes disguised, sometimes life-giving, sometimes life-disrupting presence through each season. Are these poems about the Sun? No, these verses celebrate the Sun and how she divulges and clarifies beauty and wisdom. The collection concludes with celestial dances celebrating a lyrical coalescence of cosmic lights and seasons.

When the Sun Was a Poet

Do you remember when the Sun was a poet?
Did you know her then?
The lyrical way she dappled the earth
by whispering through the trees?
The rhapsodic way she poured out daily love poems,
pink and orange and gold
into the edge of the sea?

Do you remember when the Sun was a poet?
Did you know her then?
The way she smiled warmth in winter
and called sugar snap peas out
from sleepy soil in springtime?
The way she pushed aside twilight's curtains
to serenade an autumn dawn?

Do you remember when the Sun was a poet
prophet
priest
infinite poems
plummeting
through cosmic mysteries
to laud
a million minuscule miracles
every day?

Or did we never know her? Never
really see how her luminous rhymes
burnished patches of green earth
buried now beneath
summer-hot asphalt?

Do you remember when the Sun was a poet?
Did you know her then?
But wait.
Pushing through
the cracking-open concrete
a wildflower
and a child
light-kissed
squatting close
to listen—

I. Spring's Dawning Cry

Sowing Kisses into the Wind

She squats.
Bright eyes spotlight
hose-dampened dirt.

What is it? I ask.
Without taking her eyes
off the hushful earth,

she cups her hands
and whispers
to the loamy sod—

"Grow!"
and she sows a kiss
into the un-wintering wind.

Snow Peas

Pull the loose thread and a seam opens up
Tiny canoes cradling crispy sweetness
Float into sun-warming days
Make winter vanish with a crunchy snap
Into an explosion of springtime goodness

caterpillar stitches

she
fashioned by the fashioning one
whirs and chirs
snips and clips
        weary-wise fingers offering
        this scrap of amber muslin
            that fragment of tawny linen
        to the toothy feed dog
    of her mama's singer sewer model 301a
    coaxing and cajoling the old fly-wheel
    to join bits and pieces together one more time

all other eyes in the house
on the street
shuttered tight
she beholds with tender gaze
thread that dances and dips
beneath the material surface
a winter-pale moon kissing her hands
while her love-burnished needle
marches into the wee hours
to finish a daughter's sunflower dress "just like
the one in the glossy newsstand magazine
please"

chrysalis strands spool
at dawn's unfurling edge while
she
fashioned by the fashioning one
turns the wheel one more round
and with caterpillar wisdom
stitches in a weak seam

Mockingbird Remix

Fierce.
Fire-rimmed eyes.
Zorro. Slashing, slicing.
"Nobody messes with my babies."

A suitor croons.
Twenty 4 seven. Mimus Polyglottus.
Late night urban rapper man.
Drab-suited hip hop imitator. He covers
100 tunes.
Blackbirds.
Barn swallows.
Sirens. Screeching
tires. Alarming cars.
No song his own. His voice
for her
alone.
"Nobody messes with my babies."

Fierce.
Perched
on leafy high horse.
Diving.
Swooping.
Back off, backyard beagle!
Two-ounce feather and beak projectile.
Whizzing.
Whirring.
Battle crying.
"Nobody messes with my babies."

Birth.
Fuzzy head ruffling
awake to the world.
She stands guard.
He serenades.
Nestling
solos.
"Nobody messes with my babies."

in the eye of the beholder

i lingered in their presence—

our front yard irises

pointing toward heaven
in praise of a not-yet springtime.

if only i could believe with their verdant certainty.

stems only so far
eschatological rays of color
on winter's canvas

but more than a promise

their wordless whimsical spirit-dance
part of an ancestral end-of-winter pledge
to rise up from frozen ashes
a dazzling, swirling inflorescence, a
prismatic waterfall of cavorting colors,
a backyard ballroom of blushing dancers,
silken gowns billowing in the wind,
a floral resurrection from the sleeping earth

i smile—to see a sacred wonder before its time—

could it be hope's rhizome,
en-lightened
in the iridescent iris of
a beholder?

with our eyes on the sparrows

keep your eye on the sparrows
she says as she watches my face

burrowed into church eaves
nesting in the backyard camellia bush

fence picket perchers fussing in
damp dirt behind a too-full rain catcher

no stand-out solo serenades or fiery
flashes like cardinals in springtime

no soaring hawk-winged shadow puppets
sickling dew-drenched summer grass

a copper coin for a pair of sparrows
jesus said as he watched their faces

the creating-one knows every wing-beat
fashions and fastens every feather

delights in each hair on each head
relishes every strand silvered by winter suns

i watched today as a plucky sparrow
sat on the deck rail and watched me

i imagined being able to fly away—
to escape sorrows gone viral

she nods a gentle blessing
i think i'll keep my eye on you

Letter to Last Spring's Robin

You find an old house
In the middle of the road in the rain
Water-soaked and out of place
Your eyes dart here, there, here again
You take, well, just a piece
Who will even notice
The diminishment of an old house
In the rain and out of place
The next day you come again
Just to see who is standing watch
But no one seems to care
Even though the sun
Catches drops of leftover rain
And sets them afire with light
So you dare
To snag another piece
And the next day another,
A lease, you think, on a new place
Repurposed architecture stolen away
Until only an unrecognizable fragment is left
On that last day, you dance away
Into the camellia tree by the deck
Where the terrier comes and goes
Without even noticing
The new house you've been fashioning
From an old house
Abandoned in the middle of the road in the rain

rocking chair

the tree shudders
leans forward
bends over backward

collapses

with a fire-cracking boom
hurls last years
nests to the ground

lightning takes a bow
skitters away
and grandpa heads outside

to pay his respects to the fallen one

i look at him
looking at the tree
rubbing a crooked finger

and calloused thumb along the rim
of his sweat-stained
international harvester cap—

it was magic

or so the story is told
how one spring grandpa
charmed that wounded tree
into granting him

seven slats curved
to ease an aching back
two sturdy rests for
work-weary forearms
a pair of swaying rockers

to nest grandma
who nested babies who
cradled the magic for

seeing rocking chairs in trees

Tombstone Tales

I went to see her new headstone
and the gate was open, just a crack.
Did someone sneak in

or out—

Cement kings and queens,
knights and pawns too
plot a springtime resurrection of
memories in repose
> Grandpa wearing his best Sunday suit
> Ephremia Myers lying down
> next to her only child
> (born September 6, 1885,
> died October 4, 1991)
> Uncle Lock and Aunt Mary
> side by side
> they always are—

I turn to leave,
muddy handprints
—dust to dust—
on my jeans
satisfied
mama is at rest

Or is she—

I key in the number to
Lady's Funeral Home:
"There's no death date
on my mother's tombstone.
What should I do?"

Indeed.

II. Summer's Sun-Soaked Rhapsody

sacramental season

summertime nectar magic
sweetening a vermillion-
blooming honeysuckle lamp

moscato magic
staining a glass thimble
at sunday's sacred meal
in the lutheran church
with the red door

mama's daddy
(i am his spitting image mama said)
was buried out back long before
i sat with mrs hartwell
and my own daddy
on the very last pew
watching mama's curly-permed head
sway as her feet tap-danced
handel's magic water music
on ancient pipe organ pedals

my spit-shiny mary janes tap-danced too
in the spirited air above the hardwood floor
while I waited each sunday
for daddy to come back
from the enchanted table
where he ate and drank something
that made him smell funny when
i touched his tweed jacket sleeve
and he shushed down at me
—no talking—whispering either

i was grown up enough i was sure
        (i could read chapter books
           and ride without training wheels
           and pull open the heavy doors
           of our sky blue catalina
           without daddy's help)
to taste those sweet solemn secrets
of tall waxy candlesticks
and sunlight caught in a stained glass
window given "back when"
in memory of grandpa
who's waiting out back
for grandma to come home
to that grassy chess board cemetery
where almost-forgotten aunts and uncles
are queens and kings
of as-yet unresurrected secrets

and that summer i did
drink a thimbleful of adulthood
        (or so pastor robert said
           when he showed us the
           bits of jesus and miniature
           goblets that hold
           the blood of our Lord—he
           seemed so certain of it all)
and the single sweet violet drop
stained my lips with memories
i still taste today
as if for the first time

summertime nectar
magic in a honeysuckle lamp

Red Deck Chairs on an Old Back Deck

I sat myself down
in the new red chair
on the old weather-wearied deck.
Dogs played in summer-stale grass,
wise only to the joys of a June day.
A bountiful beagle,
a tiny terrier,
they love an audience
for their long-running afternoon performances.

I attended death earlier today,
Not because a calendar marked the date and time,
but because death and I?
We arrived at the hospital together,
schedules synchronized
by my first day on the job as on-call chaplain
and by a patient's struggle with cancer.

Sadness perfumed the room,
an aroma all tangled up
with the fierce balm of undying love.
She is his best friend.
Together
from 15 years old to 67 and more.
Until.
Death showed up
and I did too
to hear a love story, to
catch a daughter's tears
in a too-small prayer.

Dogs dancing
bounding
barking at birds and squirrels,
bugs and bunnies.

A solo hummingbird
darting
dancing
delighting in a water-sugar feast.
You and me
at rest
together in the summer sun
in red deck chairs on an old back deck.

dark roast on a summer sabbath

i sip dark roast on a summer sabbath
afternoon in a bakery on 4th street downtown

alone but not by myself as voices hum all
around to the percussive café cadence of

baristas blending and brewing "basil
strawberry lemonade with just a hint

of hibiscus" and mystical "magical coffee" lactose
free but are we when no one lives forever and

too many meet death daily just outside
on 4th or 5th or another byway in this or

that town where sabbath means no
paycheck and no bread for the table tonight

a dog bark from across the way intrudes
on the poem i am scrawling and i look up

to see a tail-wagging retriever with just a hint
of something else lean in close to a bearded

man sitting cross-legged with his army duffel
in the portal of a boarded-up apartment building

where growing up through the sidewalk just in front
a sanguine dandelion waits to be held in a tiny fist

and offered as a sacred gift as precious and
precarious and persistent as life as we know it

Colors Against the Night

We sit side by side on the top deck step,
the tiny terrier and I,
and consider the summer stars.

Pyrotechnic seamstresses
pierce heaven's veil with fire-tipped needles,
stitch prismatic threads into a murky sky.
Are bottle rockets and bombastic music symphonious?

Behold! A plane crawls across the shrouding fabric
behind the embroidering spray,
wingtip strobes whirling.
What else swims and swirls out there?

A salvo trembles the earth beneath our feet.
Guns, bombs, sonic booms of grief trouble the air we breathe;
lives topple to the ground.
When will we draw silence from our pockets, fire its colors against
the night?

I look at the terrier, she at me.
A siren wails. She throws her head back
and howls and howls.

Summer Dance

She watches him across the leafy expanse,
dapper elegance bedazzling her eyes.
Ah, that vermillion bowtie pulsates
just so in the afternoon sunlight
as his heart flutters.
She hums. He notices.
Daring dancers they chassé in mid-air,
needle-pointing fireworks against pale blue skies.
Then, thirsty, they drink,
sweet scarlet sage sustaining
their buzzing tête-à-tête.
The terrier and I sit on the backyard deck.
She harrumphs. They ignore her
beguiled
oblivious
to all but each other and
the dulcet nectar of
another Cinderella summer ball.

a storied plot in a summertime backyard

i froze
jabbed
and jabbed again
by an angry dervish
jacketed in buttercup and black

then i ran
arms flailing
shirt flinging
woman alarmed
inhabited by a holy ghost buzz

i froze
stunned
swatted
and swatted again
by a wild-haired dervish
inhabited by disrobed pandemonium

then i dove
bombarded
harpooned
fury unleashed
hive mind stirred

later, ice melts
into infuriated welts
that script an epic poem
telling of an awe-full
cosmic beauty that
lures us all over again
arms and legs stinging
into the storied plot
of our untamed backyard

the white and silver hearse

parked in front of our house
this morning bumper to
bumper with steve our lawn guy's
ford f-150 that pulls a trailer
of mowers and weed-eaters
through our summertime
neighborhood streets that's what
life is like when you live
next door to a church where
people attend funerals and
weddings and sometimes
are even baptized
into new life in the side yard
in a water-filled tin trough
while you watch across
the top of your privacy fence
and from your back deck you
can hear funeral hymns offer
a counter melody to the
mower as steve fashions patterned
lines in our backyard plot
while people in their houses
up and down the block eat
their lunchtime peanut butter
and jelly sandwiches
and catch prime-time
headlines and inhale the
emerald smells of grass just
cut just outside their windows
where neighbors walk their
tiny terriers and smiling
golden retrievers and buy

cookies and flavored popcorn
from local scouts and
sometimes join funeral
processions all in the same
week because life and
death are like that
sometimes weary
combatants and sometimes
reluctant dance partners a
white and silver hearse
parked in front of my house
today and as it carried
a life remembered away
from the church to
the burial place i
knelt down
picked a bent blade
of grass and
whispered
what i hope was
a prayer

Hummingbird Blessing

She buzzes around my head,
looks me in the eye: "What, no
food? I'm hungry!" So

I replenish the feeder while
she watches from aloft the hickory
tree. Then she dives in, sonic speed

fidget spinner wings suspending her
in mid-air to drink and drink. And
my eyes drink in too as the frictionless

freedom of those unbound bits of
heaven flutter and flash and sanctify
the heavy summer air with mystery.

III. Autumn's Luminescent Lyric

First Day of Autumn

Will she visit again?
A final farewell,
a last sip of September's sweet nectar?

The air trembles,
buzzes.
She dances into view,
a blur of wings, restless
to thread opalescent color
into a seasoning sky.

She ventures closer,
levitates.
Our eyes meet.
We know.
Summer has darted away
and so must she. She flashes
away too, up onto a tree branch,
zooms in again,
pauses,
and is gone,
benediction pronounced.

Be blessed.
Until we meet again.

A Ginkgo at Thanksgiving

She lulls me
onto her halcyon dance floor
butterfly fans swirling
sun-kissed before twirling
                down
                          down
to brighten autumn's browning earth

"How many Thanksgiving dawnings
have you goldened? I ask
the wrinkled keeper of
ancestral driftings
                skitterings
                          plummetings
yellowed leaves history-haunted

Wizened Maidenhair, friend of dinosaurs
Hiroshima's living legacy and neighbor to
rush hour suburbanites, I marvel
yet again to witness your spectacular falling
                        relinquishing
                                surrendering
entrusting your harvest to cemetery sidewalks

She invites me to her ritual of
remembrance and return
each leaf giving its journey to the next
spring greening
              resurrecting
                      new-birthing
I say "yes" and abandon myself to the dance

Harvest Gifts

Bread.
Sourdough.
Pumpernickel.
Rye.
Old standbys—wheat and white.
Bread.
The stuff of life.
We break it, eat it,
Think almost nothing of it.
Golden-crusted loaves
Seasoned by the smell of the earth
Passed from me to you to the stranger.
We cannot live without it—
The bread or the sharing.
Grace.

Wine.
Poetry bottled and decanted.
Kiss of sweet grace on thirsty lips.
Wine.
Remembrance seasoned
By the taste of the earth.
Spilled out between us,
For us,
You and me and the stranger.
We cannot live without it—
The sip of mystery or the sharing.
Grace.

Water.
Trickling.
Surging.
Moaning.
Water.
We bathe in it, fear it,
Plunge its murky depths.
Washing over weary feet,
Soaking chafed hands.
We cannot live without it—
The brooding Spirit,
Sea-lapped promises on sun-singed shores.
Grace.

Bread. Wine. Water.
The earth.
Broken.
Poured out.
Stirred up
In us.
Remembering that does not forget
Hungry, wilderness people
In neighborhoods, towns, cities.
Bread. Wine. Water.
Our hands
Baking, pouring, washing.
Gifts of the earth for the people of the earth.
Grace.

October Offering

"What was that?"
Reverse. Gears grinding. Back up the mountain.
An owl. Fuzzy-headed. Too young to be wise.
Inert eyes skyward.
Bo squats. Leans in close.
"I'm not sure she will make it."
Too much lost. An inner vitality fractured.
We stare. Gawk, like people
who want to do but don't know what.
"We can't just leave it." My words startle me.
But nothing happened,
the wide-eyed three of us
breathing but not moving.
"Well?" Then an owl
in a baseball cap in my lap
in a Jeep on a mountain road
heading toward—"Stop! It's trying to fly."
Six eyes bolt. Bo hits the brakes
on the roadside again, the three of us.
I lift my offering to dusk-singed clouds.
Fly. Please.
Wings murmur.
Lanky-armed pines shiver
as the October wind catches up
and the tawny sky
welcomes the owl home
as we watch from the side of the road.

ode to a sycamore

the tree fell
crashed with a thud
or perhaps
a tympanic
boom—lumberjacked
supercentenarian
ancestral truth encrypted
in woody rings now exposed

blaze of autumn beauty
provisional performance platform
for yellow-browed warblers
darting from one leafy branch to another
promised spring nesting place
now gone and up there
in the deprived autumn sky
a lonely swallow circles—

Ashes to Ashes

No one knew where she came from—
sprung up out of the soil
where her daddy's farmhouse was planted?
Blew in with the fragrance of gran's roses?

Tumbled from the clouds in a thunderstorm, more likely.

When she died we scattered her ashes
in the bluebonnet patch by the pond
guided by rays of a setting sun.

She'd left instructions in her will—well
on an old napkin from the cafe downtown.
the essence of her liminal life,

I didn't expect the wind to dance that evening.
But just as we released her ashes,
a breeze blew up a puff of silver-white into
my face
hair
eyelashes.

"Maybe she'll grow back
now that we've planted her," my sister laughed
as the ashes settled

But we knew who had the last laugh—
growing ghosts from winter ground
that was her specialty.

I wore her red silk scarf that day—
to be close to her.
Vinegar and raspberries—the scent of her voice.

Now she—the rootless floating one—
seasons my hair,
tickles my nose,
and I laugh into the wind
as a waning moon wanders
up over fiery autumn trees.

Winter Prelude

Holly's berries were green
then pinkish orange,
color deepening now
with each day the
sun sleeps longer. The
berries impersonate Mama's

shade-shifting lipstick, I
think, waxy green in the
tube, transformed to candy
apple red on her lips. "Don't
you think you're overdoing it,

a bit?" I asked Holly. I have
never seen so many berries.
She must be getting tired from
wearing all the jewels summer
has draped over her spindly arms.

Her only response is to blush
in the autumn light while Mama
Wren sticks her head out from
the inflamed branches and offers
up a scolding winter prelude

IV. Winter's Silver-Sheened Silences

Cedars in Snowy Places

Winter.
Solstice.
Gyroscopic dance
choreographed by Earth's axial tilt.
Sun stand still
Longest night
shortest day
Yule
Midwinter
The land is vulnerable now,
sometimes covered by snowflakes
that have let go of something
somewhere
up there
pirouetted down
down,
down
from the heavens
to enchant
rooftops
leaning-over farm fences
autumn-tarnished grass.
And while tulip bulbs repose
in unseen silence
beneath the austere earth,
cedars in snowy places
fragrance the cold air
with emerald stillness
and praise the December moonlight.

Upon a Midnight

Light.
They say
the angel-sparked kind
startled keeping-watch
shepherds in the fields
all those years ago—
did we relegate that light
to the attic along with
the olive wood crèche
from the Holy Land
Mama bought at Biltmore House
that year to put on
the piano but that is
now missing its wise people?

That shepherding light—
is it little more than
a relic from dimmer days
before electric stars studded
the night skies,
when we knew
we needed at the ready
oil-drenched wicks,
trimmed and burning,
to spread light out
upon sable-saturated shores?

Is that light just
a quaint idea crooned
by somnolent voices repeating
old Christmas tunes
about holy nights suspended
over a longed-for little
town that is noisy now
with peace distrupted?

Picturesque promises won't do
in a world of portraits
painted in innocent blood
and unsustainable oils.
How did we let ourselves
get hoodwinked by
fluorescent foolishness?

Right here,
now,
upon a midnight
an obligato flame flickers
just ahead where the
half-spent day
gave up the ghost—
but we cannot
give up.
Let us turn our feet toward
the light and go
one more time
upon our way.

i want my feet to tell me

i want my feet to tell me
where i stand because they
remember where we have walked

i want gravel to crunch beneath
my shoes and silence to fall like
winter snow when my steps are stilled

stolen by a quicksilver flash of
recognition in a not-so-stranger's eyes
as we pass by each other on the way

i want unexplored dreams to draw
me to stones as yet unturned on
unfamiliar roads longing to be

touched by the tread of toes
tender enough to delight in the
tickle of eternal seeds of dust

i want a honeyed light in the kitchen
in that house on 38th street to burn
through the fog so i won't get lost on

my pilgrimage to overhear somebody's
grandma telling about the time she
or was it i got saved on her front porch

i want my feet to tell me
where i stand because they
remember where we have walked

a murder of stillness

they murdered the stillness and
hid the remains in the snow-bent
branches of our backyard cedar

that is what the terrier and i witnessed as
raucous squawking mobbed our ears
barking beaks devouring chunks of silence

are they a ravenous hitchcockian coven
come to marble the winter-grim skies with
their menacing mass or are they only hunting

a nighttime perch as the dying sun's
blood-red rays pierce crystalline-cocooned
bird feeders standing empty in the chill air

perhaps if we were fluent in their rambunctious
yawps and caws we would guffaw with them at
whatever wicked joke has tickled their feathers

but the tiny terrier was having none of that
tearing off the deck in a furied flurry flinging an
incensed growl up into the obsidian-flecked trees

then with a synchronized flap of great noisy
wings they were no more and quiet fell unadorned
as a deserted feather onto the sleeping ground

silenced snow globe

reindeer perpetually landed
on the rooftop of the house
inside aunt julia's snow globe

the little girl on the road out
front never stopped gazing
toward the festive front door

and I never let the snow
stop rising up and falling
back down inside that dome

i held the weather in my hand
and could orchestrate a tiny
winter wonderland all my own

dreaming of christmas eve
sleigh bells chiming merry gladness
outside my little yellow bedroom

cloudiness now obscures
the constructed cheery
panorama in that globe

no more swirling snow
stalled reindeer
magic evaporated

and the girl—
toppled over
something about her

broken i shake the globe
shake it again and keep vigil
for a world trapped in winter

winter pilgrimage

winter weeps and wails
covering her tracks as
she races wild and fast
down the beach where
an orange umbrella presses
itself flat against wood pilings
to let her pass—

mama and her little one
sheltered once beneath
that pummeled parasol
to build summertime palaces
now besieged by salty snow
that soaks into the tide
and drifts away—

and all the while celestial
diadems cocoon within
storm-expectant clouds
for some reason not ready to
blossom forth so that she might
gather their astral blooms to
light her winterward way—

mama walks into the gale anyway
cradling her child while
one hand clasps to her head the
purple hat she had hoped might
defend against the howling cold but
instead threatens to fly away into
the night chasing sandcastle stars—

January Epiphanies

Star-watchers.
Eyes wide opened
by what they see
in backyard night skies,
a dream and a LED-bright star their GPS,
"Bearing gifts they traverse afar"
to investigate
explore
consider.

Then—eyes wide opened
by what they see—
re-routed,
home by another way.

Ah, the peculiarity of Christmastide epiphanies:
shepherds
cows and sheep and donkeys
an angel-touched teenager
and a dream-visited carpenter
sky-gazing Zorastrians
on camel's backs
tracing a celestial light-beam to a distant place.

But what of the rest of the story?
Menacing messages from powerful places
the slaughter of innocents,
mama and daddy,
baby held tight
fleeing
violence
death.
Did they know—
to keep their bodies safe
was to keep safe
fierce-fragile hope?

In all of it—
holy visits and visions and vistas
detours and dancing stars
midnight border crossings
into unfamiliar backyards
the kindnesses of strangers
children's cries
wailing lullabies
"Hush, little baby! Don't say a word"
somehow?
Heralded by the morning song
of an ordinary
brown-feathered barn-bird
Immanuel—hope-with-us.

Galactic light-spheres align yet again.
A winter sun arises
shines
burns away the fog of unknowing
and eyes wide-opened
by what we see,
hope leaps in daylight wombs
and we labor once more
to birth
life
love
illumination.

V. Celestial Dances

Daffodil Prayers

"Dip your aching toes
in cool waters,"
said Summer to the
wilderness
wandering
woman.

"Tease your tastebuds
with blackberries. Lay
your weary body down
on gentle meadow
grass. Breathe in the
soft sweetness of coral
honeysuckle where
hummingbirds drink
and dance."

"Blush with pride,"
said Autumn
to the old maple tree.
"You earned it.
Shaded the little girl who
held summer stars
in her eyes
while she
sat beneath your branches
and read
and read
and read
once upon a times into
dreams into
fierce hopes for the future."

"Bend toward hope
when icy winds blow,"
said Winter
to the fragile-seeming ones.
"Bend, but don't break.
You are stronger than you know.
You are resilient.
You are enough."

"To push your shoulders
up, up, up,"
said Spring.
"Up through still-cold
greening sod to
fragrance the dawn
with daffodil prayers.

On Not Chasing Time

We usually chase time,
scrambling down
into an hour-glass ravine
while loose rocks
slide beneath hurry-up feet.

What if—we stop skimming the surface
of others on our way
to countless wherevers?
What if we hug our lives.
Remember how real they are,
flesh and blood from dust
returning to dust

What if—we who once watched the world
through a calendar-grid of windows,
uncoiled life in slower-motion?
    dogwood flags unfurl
    two cardinals meet talk
    flirt measure each other up
    marry their lives
    in the too-berried
    holly too-close to the house
    bush beans in a new bed
    worry their heads up
    through unfamiliar soil
    while bumblebees samba
    mid-air until sunset when
    a pregnant pink moon rests
    in the crook of the lean-to maple
    out back where a squirrel sits
    to nibble last year's pecans

What do I owe time?

A waltz.

to "watch again another night"

(after Walt Whitman)

can we watch again another night

for celestial wonders
to rise up
somehow
somewhere
out of a cradle
of ashes?

can we watch again another night

for the sacred star-flinger
to transgress apocryphal boundaries
and sow into the sky
upon a midnight clear
a blossoming Bethlehem blessing?

we stumble in dark places
where stars have
come crashing down
with a bomb blast
or a mother's wail or
a whisper in a waiting room.

can we watch again another night?

for dawn's endearing face to caress
our weary waiting eyes with hope?

Newborn Lullabies

I am his heart,
the beat
beat beating heart.
Perhaps you have seen photographs.
Such a peaceful visage. Still
unravaged
by the beat beat beating
of time.
A hawk-moth hummingbird mid-air
suspended
in the picture window
trembles
spirals
down
to kiss a moonflower's awakening ear,
pulse
quickening
as nectar of paradise
thrums through quivering wings.
A nurse,
eleventh hour of a twelve hour shift,
pauses. Looks out through the window
exhales
turns inward. Tender
eyes alight on his face.
She touches two fingers
to a small wrist.
She counts my pulsating surges
one two,
three four
thirteen fourteen fifteen

Mama cradles the child whose
body cradles me. I am
his heart.
Suspended in a tornado's eye. Still.
She hears me
as another night ascends and
falling rain begins to
beat beat beat
on the window pane.

vital signs

her chart is heavier than she is,
an out-of-print catalogue of diminishing

vital signs

blood pressure monitor
beep, beep, beeping

sun-washed backyard beagle
battling sleep on a springtime afternoon

ice-tipped thermometer
seeking out the underside of a tongue

toasted coconut ice cream
overflowing a summer sugar cone

oxygen breathing life
into somnolent veins

dinner by candlelight
heart rate racing

code blue, north tower
monitor beep, beeping, beep

rainbow arms
cradling storm clouds in their sleep

jagged lines
treasures and secrets exposed

her vitality evaporates
through chiffon skin

frail (i am convinced)
until she grasps my hand

Beneath Our Feet, In Our Hands

Jack Frost is curled up, napping
In my bones.
Backyard grass crunches, frozen
Beneath my feet.
Summer sunflowers hibernate, silent
In my heart.

Could it be—
When I hold this dried out husk
Springtime rests on wintertide fingertips?
Infinitesimal harbinger of arugula and radishes;
Holder of stories—fields plowed,
Dirt collected under ungloved fingernails.
Death—in autumn—
Birth—in spring—
When tender-strong seedlings
Unfurl from soil-stained shells,
And push through the earth
Gasping for the sun—

Dirt weeps sometimes too,
And calls to us: We are stronger than we imagine.
Justice—in wilderness places—
Freedom—in a kernel—
An orchard redeemed—blossoming
Sweet succulent promises of life overflowing.

So we take our shoes off to
Absorb holy ground nutrients
Beneath our feet.
And we water with salt-seasoned tears
This garden we hold in our hand.

harvesting ancient sunrises

we walk each day among the trees
feet steadied by land not ours alone
ground made sacred by others
soil sunlit by dawns before our birth
sown with with ancient stories
watered by lamenting
rejoicing
splashing
soaking
sweat and tears
springtimes harvested
from hardscrabble winters

Dear Midnight,

Who do you talk to
when the wrens and robins
go quiet in a storm?
You know, when lightning
strikes every city in every land
and ignites down deep darkness?

The tiny terrier and I
cock our heads—
She growls down deep
in her belly suspicious
at not hearing electricity
scurry through the house.

Rain tiptoes toward us
then chases us home,
silken hair flying out behind her.
She slips in with us as the
door slams with a sonic boom
and a single metallic flash of light—

Silence sidles in too,
scampers off into corners
and down deep into crevices
and we all peer out the window
at a sky homesick for stars.

Dear Midnight
Can you tell us what it all means?
You, who wander fields and forests
seeking the fierce feeble embers
of once-fiery mornings—

The tiny terrier and I cock our heads.
Out there—
in the dripping down deep darkness
a train whistle melts
into the rain-slick trees
and a barn owl queries the night.

Saving a Dance for Me

It's been too long, old friend,
since I last luxuriated in your dance—
not because you weren't moving
but because my eyes were
too full of distracting debris
to see your music.
Ancient rocks welcome your embrace.
Pebbles flash brilliant smiles
as you caress their backs.
And trees lean in close
to share your whispered secrets.
Thank you for continuing
to cascade
stretch
twirl
leap
to the music of the spheres.
Thank you—
for saving a dance
for me.

The Other Half of the Sky

"See? That's the Big Dipper.
And the Little Dipper is over there."

We watched the autumn night sky together,
Dad and I. I wanted to see what he saw—

Stories in the stars. Fiery folktales of
kings, queens and chameleons;

a lizard, a lynx, and a lion.
Celestial chronicles scripted onto

a black velvet picture book.
I longed to read the stars where

a deranged dragonfish hurtles
toward the earth from two million

miles away. What cosmic superhero
will rise to the challenge? I asked

my dad as he tucked me and
my beagle Hunter into our bed:

"And what is a 'lesser dog' by the way?"
Still the astronomical plot eludes

me. Eludes us—if we are wise to
perceive: star-storying? A singular distillation

of collective imagination. Parabolic patterns
premised on where our lives are planted.

Forever made mystical, magical even,
by remembering—when on a clear night

we think we can see forever? The star
so blazing brilliant to our naked eye

burned out yesterday, and always—always—
half the sky is hidden away beneath our feet.

Epilogue: the sun is a poet

the sun is poet
scripting light
into shaded gardens
where wonder-working worms
wriggle
beneath the soil

the moon waxes eloquent
bashful ballad one moment
bold supernova the next
performing light
on a gyrating intergalactic stage

maybe fireflies are bards too
and grasshoppers and hummingbirds
and gravel that crunches
when you walk on it
and who can forget
pine trees and penguins
and parrots with plumes
dipped in glistening glass green

my bent nib fountain pen listens
leans close
releases
spidery webs to
capture
the next verse

About the Author

Jill Crainshaw is a poet, professor, and preacher. When she is not teaching at Wake Forest University School of Divinity in Winston-Salem, NC, she and her two pups, Bella and Penny, look for poems in their backyard. Sometimes Jill writes them down.

Through her writing and teaching, Jill celebrates life's seasons and seasonings. Jill has authored seven academic books in her spirituality, theology, and religious leadership disciplines. Her poetry can be found in several journals and magazines, including *Synkoniciti, The New Verse News,* and *Writing in a Woman's Voice.*

www.ingramcontent.com/pod-product-compliance
Lightning Source LLC
Chambersburg PA
CBHW071011160426
43193CB00012B/2010